Affirmation Book

FOR TEENS AND YOUNG ADULTS

EMPOWERING WHO YOU ARE

by Steve Viglione

Graphic Design and Illustration:
Mauricio Hoffman
and Ashikurim Enelkuraham

Layout by 1106 Design

English-Spanish Edition

© 2011 Steve Viglione, All rights reserved
Published by The I AM Foundation
www.iamfoundation.org

Sponsored by:

Jodi Hronis
Advocate for Teens and Young Adults
and
The I AM Foundation's
Points of Light Campaign Donors

I AM!
And I am made from Love,
Which also made the rainbow,
The flower, the sea, the dove.

⊱✦⊰

Yo Soy!
Y estoy hecho de amor,
El cual también hizo el arco iris,
La flor, el mar, la paloma.

I Am!
And with everything I am One,
The plants, the trees, the animals,
The stars, the moon, the sun.

Yo Soy!
Y con todo yo soy uno,
las plantas, los árboles, los animales,
las estrellas, la luna y el sol.

I Am Priceless!
There's nothing worth more than me,
Whether it's the whole world,
Or the smallest thing you can see.

Yo Soy Invaluable!
Y no hay nada con más valor que yo,
Así sea el mundo entero,
O la cosa más pequeña que se pueda ver.

I Am Greatness!
I know others are Greatness too.
If you ask me about yourself,
I will tell you, so are you.

Yo Soy Grandioso!
Y sé que otros son Gradioso también,
Si me preguntas de ti,
Te diré que tu también lo eres.

I Am Infinite!
Inside me there is a treasure.
Of gifts I can give to everyone,
Too countless to even measure.

Yo Soy Infinito!
Dentro de mí hay un tesoro,
De regalos que les puedo dar a cada uno,
Demasiados para poder contar.

I Am Worthy!
So there is nothing here on earth,
That can keep me from my Good,
Or take away my worth.

Yo Soy Valioso!
No hay nada en este mundo,
Que me separe de lo Mío
O me quite el valor.

I Am Joy!
And everywhere I go,
People have to stop,
To appreciate my glow.

Yo Soy Alegría!
Y a dondequiera que voy,
La gente se detiene
Para apreciar mi gozo.

I Am Proud!
And so I stand up tall.
I give a smile to everyone,
As I greet them all.

Yo Soy Orgulloso!
Y me paro derecho
Y le sonrío a todo el mundo
Al saludarlos a todos.

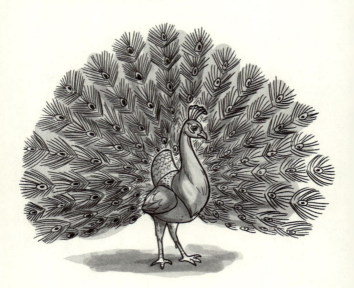

I Am Powerful!
Because of the Greatness that's in me,
It's the truth of who I am,
The truth I am to be.

Yo Soy Poderoso!
Por la grandeza que ha en mí,
Es la verdad de quien soy,
La verdad seré.

I Am Strong!
And I know how unique I am.
I have what it takes,
To be the Me I am.

Yo Soy Fuerte!
Y sé que tan especial soy,
Tengo lo que se necesita
Para ser quien Soy Yo.

I Am Vision!
Seeing the Plan that's in store for me,
I listen when I'm quiet,
To my heart that holds the key.

Yo Soy Visión!
Al ver el plan que me espera,
Escucho cuando estoy en silencio,
A mi corazón que guarda la llave.

I Am Somebody!
Yes, Somebody I Am!
And I can see a dream in me,
It's part of that great Plan.

Yo Soy Alguien!
Sí, Alguien Soy!
Y puedo ver un sueño en mí,
Es parte de un gran Plan.

I Am Confidence!
Regardless of what others say or do,
I simply believe in myself,
And the Dream I've set my mind to.

Yo Soy Confianza!
A pesar de lo que otros digan o hagan,
Simplemente creo en mí mismo,
Y en el sueño que he decidido.

I Am Patience!
And even if I think things go wrong,
I know inside me very well,
They'll turn around before too long.

Yo Soy Paciencia!
Y aún si pienso que algunas coas van mal,
Sé muy bien dentro de mí,
Que todo va a mejorar muy pronto.

I Am Success!
And what I start I sure can do.
I simply practice, practice, practice,
The Thing I've set my mind to.

Yo Soy Éxito!
Y lo que empiezo lo puedo hacer,
Simplemente practico, practico, practico,
Las Cosas que decido hacer.

I Am Excellence!
And if it's a mistake I think I've made,
I can learn a lot from it,
To help the Plan I've laid.

Yo Soy Excelencia!
Y si un error creo haber hecho,
Aprendo mucho de él,
Para ayudar al plan que he establecido.

I Am Wholeness!
And I Love the body that I'm in.
I accept myself and others.
When I come from Love I win.

Yo Soy Completo!
Y me encanta el cuerpo en el que estoy,
Me acepto a mí mismo y a los demás,
Siempre gano todo con amor.

I Am Honest!
And if we disagree,
I talk about my feelings,
Respecting You as well as Me.

Yo Soy Honesto!
Y si no estamos de acuerdo,
Hablamos de mis sentimientos,
Respetandote e Tí como a Mí.

I Am Persistence!
I face my fears head on.
And as I stand to face them,
One by one they're gone.

Yo Soy Persistente!
Le hago frente a mis temores,
Y al darles la cara,
Uno a uno desaparecen.

I Am Brave!
And I allow myself to feel,
Each feeling that I have,
It's part of being real.

Yo Soy Valiente!
Y me permito sentir,
Cada sentimiento que tengo
Es parte de ser verdadero.

I Am Attractive!
And I make friends and be,
The Gift I am to everyone,
The Gift I am to me.

Yo Soy Atractivo!
Y hago amigos y soy,
El Regalo que soy para todos,
El Regalo que soy para mí.

I Am Helpful!
Knowing it's my hand that I can lend,
If my friend is hurting,
My Heart will help them mend.

Yo Soy Util!
Sabiendo que puedo hechar una mano,
Si mi amigo está herido,
Mi corazón le ayudará a sanar.

I Am Brilliance!
And of all the things I know,
Helping one another is the
Greatest way to grow.

Yo Soy Brillantez!
Y de todas las cosas que sé,
Ayudarse uno a otro,
Es la forma que Más hace crecer.

I Am Generous!
So the more Good I give,
The more that I receive,
And the happier I live.

Yo Soy Generoso!
Así que entre más hago el bien,
Más recibo,
Y más feliz vivo.

I Am Peaceful!
And I love the grass so green.
When I'm lying down in it,
It makes me King or Queen.

Yo Soy Pacífico!
Y me encanta el pasto tan verde,
Cuando me recuesto sobre él,
Me convierte en Rey o Reina.

I Am Freedom!
And on a breezy summer night,
I love to see the stars,
The moon, its shape, its light.

Yo Soy Libertad!
Y en la noche fresca del verano,
Me encanta ver las estrellas,
La luna, su forma, su luz.

I Am Abundance!
And in Nature I am rich,
I count its many blessings,
There's one in every niche.

Yo Soy Abundancia!
Y en Naturaleza soy rico,
Y cuento sus muchas bendiciones,
Hay una en cada rincón.

I Am Grateful!
And the way that I believe,
Is giving thanks for what I have,
And for what I will receive.

Yo Estoy Agradecido!
Y la manera en la que yo creo,
Es dar gracias por lo que tengo,
Y por lo que voy a recibir.

I Am Healthy!
Being balanced all around.
I eat good foods and exercise,
I am healthy by the pound.

Yo Soy Saludable!
Balanceado en todo aspecto,
Como bien y hago ejercicio,
Kilo a kilo tengo salud plena.

I Am Wisdom!
Thinking Good with every thought,
Being guided from within,
My direction is self-taught.

Yo Soy Sabiduría!
Con sólo buenos pensamientos,
Guiándome por lo que llevo dentro,
Mi directriz está en mí.

I Am Loving!
In each and every way.
In fact it's what I tell myself
At the start of each new day.

Yo Soy Cariñoso!
En cada uno y en toda forma,
Es lo que me digo a mí mismo,
Al comienzo de cada día.

Now I know who I Am,
And when I close my eyes I see,
The incredible person that I am,
The I Am, that is Me.

Ahora Sé quién Soy,
Y cuando cierro mis ojos veo,
El Persona increíble que soy,
Ese Ser, soy Yo.

Empowering Who You Are Through Your Own Affirmations and Sketches

If you have enjoyed the affirmations and illustrations in this book and feel inspired to write your own affirmations or draw sketches, here are some pages for you to express your brilliance and creativity.

My Own Affirmations and Sketches...

My Own Affirmations and Sketches...

My Own Affirmations and Sketches...

My Own Affirmations and Sketches...

How to "Empower Who You Are" through the Use of Affirmations

By Dr. Marilyn Powers

Affirmations are your words of power. They focus on what is good and right about you. They help you to face your fears and challenges. And they inspire you to express your talents and gifts to make a positive difference in the world.

An affirmation is a statement of positive intent; it affirms your self-worth and value.

Four ways to use an affirmation:

- Think it
- Write it
- Speak it
- Visualize it

Think an I AM! Affirmation when a negative thought comes up. Replace the negative thought with an I AM! Affirmation, i.e. a positive thought.

Write an I AM! Affirmation. Reinforce the power of the I AM! Affirmation by writing it out five times. On a page make two columns; in the column on the left write the I AM! Affirmation, and in the column on the right, write any reactions, thoughts or feelings that come up.

Speak an I AM! Affirmation. Say the affirmation out loud. When you speak the words out loud, they strengthen your self-esteem and empower you to take positive action.

Visualize an I AM! Affirmation. Put your imagination to work. Close your eyes and picture the affirmation at work in your life. Feel the feelings, picture how you look and act when you affirm the truth of the affirmation. Get a clear image of yourself affirming the I AM! Affirmation.

Choose your I AM! Affirmation for the day, the week or the month. Commit to memorizing that I AM! Affirmation. Say it out loud that day, or each day, that week or month. Remember this: "Words up, words down, a smile or a frown, the choice is mine."

How to use affirmations to empower you:

As you begin each day you can focus on what is good and right about you. Affirm out loud in the mirror or when you are dressing: *"I am strong! And I know how unique I am. I have what it takes, to be the Me I am."* Then, when walking to school or work, you can choose to affirm: *"I am powerful! Because of the greatness that's in me, it's the truth of who I am, the truth I am to be."*

Then midday, if a challenge confronts you, you can also choose to affirm: *"I am persistence! I face my fears head on and as I stand to face them, one by one they're gone."*

In the afternoon, if your feelings have been hurt, you can choose to affirm: *"I am brave! And I allow myself to feel, each feeling that I have, it's part of being real."* Or you can affirm if a friend needs your help: *"I am helpful! Knowing it's my hand that I can lend, If my friend is hurting, my heart will help them mend."*

And if you make a mistake you can choose to say: *"I am excellence! And if it's a mistake I think I've made, I can learn a lot from it, to help the plan I've laid."*

At home, when doing homework or a work project, you can affirm: *"I am success! And what I start I sure can do. I simply practice, practice, practice, The thing I've set my mind to."*

Also, before going to bed you can look back throughout the day and affirm: *"I am grateful! And the way that I believe, Is giving thanks for what I have and for what I will receive."*

Finally, before closing your eyes, choose to remember: *"Now I know who I am, And when I close my eyes I see, The incredible person that I am, The I Am that is me."*

Throughout the day your I AM! Affirmations can keep your mood up, help you overcome obstacles and, most importantly, build your self-confidence: *"I am confidence! Regardless of what others say or do, I simply believe in myself, And the dream, I've set my mind to."*

As you become more familiar with the I AM! Affirmations and even memorize them, you will be able to recall the affirmation at any point during the day. Or you can refer to your pocket edition of this book; turn to the appropriate affirmation that will support you when you need it.

You are always at choice. When you choose to take control of your life, you choose to think of and to speak the I AM! Affirmations. You have the power to feel good about yourself. Your destiny is in your hands when you choose to remember how valuable and important you are. Then together, we can create a world that serves us all.

A Message from Steve Viglione

As I sit down to write this message to you, the reader of this book, my intention is to communicate in an authentic, person-to-person way that inspires you to connect with the core of who you are.

In my teenage and young adult years, I could only partially connect with the truth of who I was. Now in my adult years, I can see more clearly who I am, and it is my intention for you that, no matter where you are on your journey, you will honor yourself and your unique talents and gifts. Honor the fact that there is a reason for your being here, even if you don't know what that reason is. It could be lying dormant or you might even know now what the reason is.

Also, when I lived through the years that you are experiencing right now, I thought I could do it all on my own and did not need anyone or anyone's advice. I was quickly humbled to learn that I do need others, and I can learn from them as well. No matter how old or young we are, we can all learn from each other.

It is important for me that you know the authors of this book are your equals, that you receive the words in this book as something positive that can support you in your daily life, and that this book was written out of deep compassion for the challenges you may face in your life, as you grow and embrace your interdependence with the world.

It is my goal for this book that you can find the value in saying positive affirmations to yourself and seeing what a difference they can make in your life.

When I first found positive affirmations and used them as a daily tool, I noticed that my energy shifted from feeling down about myself to feeling great about myself.

Too often, in the place of not feeling good about ourselves, we can attract things that can bring us down or even be destructive. I trust that as you read this and gain this awareness, something will shift for you, and your daily use of affirmations can elevate your mood and self-confidence. This in turn will support you in attracting the very best!

It is also my sincere intention that, whenever you feel challenged by a situation or person, you can remember to use the affirmations in this book, or even write affirmations that are personal to you. Let affirmations lift you up so you can be the great gift to this planet that you were born to be. The world is waiting for you; it needs you now.

—Steve Viglione
Written overlooking the ocean in Mendocino, CA
April 29, 2011

A message from
The Consul General of Sri Lanka,
Mr. Jeff M. Goonewardena

As a teenager and young adult I worked very hard in the hotel industry in Sri Lanka, where I was born and raised. Many of you might not know about Sri Lanka; it is an island nation that is a beautiful piece of paradise in South Asia in the Indian Ocean.

Over the years I had a dream and vision to come to America and be successful. I had no idea at that time that I would be fortunate enough to be the Consul General of Sri Lanka to Venezuela, Colombia and to eleven of the western states of the U.S.A.

In addition, I have done a lot of humanitarian work around the world. After the tsunami of 2004, I personally drove to the hard hit areas of the country to help my people. A few years later, I invited Steve Viglione and Dr. Marilyn Powers, of The I AM Foundation, to meet the First Lady of my country and to gift more than 100,000 copies of the children's edition of *The I AM! Affirmation Book* and school supplies to the kids who survived the disaster. In 2008, I joined Steve and Marilyn on a book gifting mission to help gift more than 50,000 books to children after Hurricane Katrina.

The reason that I share all of this with you is I want you to always believe in yourself and the vision that you have been given for your life. Even if you don't know what that is yet, everyone has a purpose here in the world. I encourage you to find out what yours is.

It would mean so much to me if anything said here inspires you in any way to live your dreams, and contributes to your vision becoming a reality. The work of Steve and Marilyn and The I AM Foundation is so important because it helps us to focus on what is good and right about us, regardless of any negative thoughts we have, or judgments from others. This book will encourage you to connect with your greatest talents and gifts so that you can contribute to a positive society now and in the future.

Very sincerely yours,

Jeff M. Goonewardena, Consul General of
Sri Lanka to Venezuela and Colombia
Former Consul General to Los Angeles, CA and
Eleven Western States in the U.S.A.
Honorary Mayor of Baton Rouge, Louisiana and
Oceanside, California

How to Order This Book

To purchase additional copies of *The I AM! Affirmation Book for Teens and Young Adults, Empowering Who You Are* in small and large quantities, please visit www.iamfoundation.org or call us at 619.297.7010.

Custom print runs are available for sponsors who would like to have their message inside this book.

Consider gifting this book at:
- Teen and Young Adult Camps
- Teen and Young Adult Conferences
- Teen and Young Adult Centers
- Schools and Colleges
- Graduations

Other Books in The Love~Wisdom Series

For Children

For ages pre-Kindergarten through 4th grade

The I AM! Affirmation Book: Discovering Who You Are English~Spanish Edition $9.95

The I AM! Affirmation eBook: Discovering Who You Are English~Spanish Edition $9.95 *(eBooks also available in French, Italian, Arabic, Farsi, Urdu, Swahili, Chinese, Tagalog, Portuguese and more)*

For ages Kindergarten through 6th grade

I Am The Earth: Positive Affirmations for Loving Our Planet English~Spanish Edition Book $12.00

I Am The Earth: Positive Affirmations for Loving Our Planet English~Spanish Edition eBook $10.00

Coming in 2012

I Am Healthy! Affirmations for Health and Well Being $9.95

I Am Healthy! Affirmations for Health and Well Being eBook $9.95

For Parents and Teachers

The I AM! Affirmation Curriculum $44.95

The I AM! Affirmation Curriculum eBook $29.95

The I Am The Earth Curriculum $44.95

The I Am The Earth eBook Curriculum $29.95

For Adults

Words of Power: Affirmations for Loving Your Age, Work and Life $14.95

Words of Power: Affirmations for Loving Your Age, Work and Life eBook $12.95

The Bridge: A Seven-Stage Map to Redefine Your Life and Purpose $16.95

The Bridge: A Seven-Stage Map to Redefine Your Life and Purpose eBook $14.95

The Bridge Companion Workbook $44.95

The Bridge Companion eWorkbook $29.95

All books available at www.iamfoundation.org, selected book sellers, Amazon.com, DeVorss Distributors or by calling The I AM Foundation at 619.297.7010.

A Recommended Read...

Empowering Teens to Build Self-Esteem
by Suzanne E. Harrill, M.Ed. LPC
ISBN 978-883648-04-6 $16.95

A quick, easy read that empowers teens to be their own best friend, to take personal responsibility, and how to re-script one's life for success and happiness. Builds positive Self-Talk. Includes affirmations, journal questions, Teen Self-Esteem Awareness Inventory and dating tips. Also for parents, teachers and counselors.

"I'm excited to see a book offering simple wisdom and critical guidance to teens. In a sensitive yet upbeat style Harrill lays out essential survival skills for teenagers, highlighting the paths leading to the heart of personal success. I wish every teenager (and parent) had this marked as required reading."

— NAPRA ReView

Meet Suzanne E. Harrill, receive a free newsletter and order books/eBooks: *www.InnerworksPublishing.com*
Available from Partners, Amazon, also on Kindle

The I AM Foundation's Points of Light Campaign

We would like to acknowledge all of
The I AM Foundation's Points of Light
who make our work possible in the world.

Our Points of Light either raise or donate funds
to help us publish and gift the books in the
Love~Wisdom Series.

For more information on how you can become
part of the Point of Lights Campaign and
help us gift this book or other books in the
Love~Wisdom Series to your community,

please visit *www.iamfoundation.org*
or call us at 619.297.7010.

How to Contact the Authors

Dr. Marilyn Powers and Steve Viglione offer inspirational programs that empower dynamic change to move you in new and positive directions. They are each available for speaking  engagements and to lead seminars to redefine your life and purpose. Marilyn and Steve work with individuals, couples and corporations, as well as youth groups and community service organizations. Philanthropic programs that create new avenues of humanitarian service both nationally and globally are offered.

For more information or to contact Marilyn or Steve, please visit www.iamfoundation.org, e-mail iam@iamfoundation.org, or contact them directly at 619.297.7010.

About The I AM Foundation

The I AM Foundation is a 501(c)3 educational non-profit organization whose mission is empowering children and adults worldwide through publishing and gifting The Love~Wisdom Series. Since the organization was founded in 1998, more than one million books and products have been gifted and distributed worldwide.

If you feel inspired by the work of The I AM Foundation, you can join us in impacting children and adults across the globe by gifting books from The Love~Wisdom Series, sponsoring book gifting missions in schools and other organizations, or by making tax-deductible contributions.

To volunteer, purchase books, sponsor a book-gifting mission, make a donation, or to learn more about The I AM Foundation, please visit www.iamfoundation.org or call 619.297.7010.